BACKALONG

Nia Broomhall won the 2023 *Mslexia* Women's Poetry Pamphlet Competition judged by Imtiaz Dharker for her debut collection *Backalong* (Bloodaxe Books/Mslexia, 2024). She received an MA with distinction in Creative Writing from Lancaster University in 2023, and is Poet in Residence at Painshill Park in Surrey for 2024, funded by an Arts Council DYCP grant. She won the Poetry Society's Hamish Canham Prize for 2023/2024, and was Highly Commended in the Winchester Poetry Prize in 2022 and 2023. Her poems have been published in *Magma, Bad Lilies, Ink, Sweat and Tears, The Alchemy Spoon, The Interpreter's House* and *The Friday Poem*, and anthologised by Sidhe Press and Black Bough Poetry. Currently co-Head of English at a comprehensive school in Surrey, the best hour of her week is Poetry Club on a Friday afternoon. Originally from rural Somerset, she comes from a long line of West Country women who talk to strangers and embarrass their children.

NIA BROOMHALL

Backalong

BLOODAXE BOOKS

Copyright © Nia Broomhall 2024

ISBN: 978 1 78037 716 2

First published 2024 by
Bloodaxe Books Ltd,
Eastburn,
South Park,
Hexham,
Northumberland NE46 1BS
in association with *Mslexia*

www.bloodaxebooks.com

For further information about Bloodaxe titles
please visit our website and join our mailing list
or write to the above address for a catalogue.

LEGAL NOTICE

All rights reserved. No part of this book may be
reproduced, stored in a retrieval system, or
transmitted in any form, or by any means, electronic,
mechanical, photocopying, recording or otherwise,
without prior written permission from Bloodaxe Books Ltd.

Requests to publish work from this book
must be sent to Bloodaxe Books Ltd.

Nia Broomhall has asserted her right under
Section 77 of the Copyright, Designs and Patents Act 1988
to be identified as the author of this work.

Cover design: Neil Astley & Pamela Robertson-Pearce.

Printed in Great Britain by PrintedEasy.com, Letchworth, Herts,
on FSC-certified Arena paper manufactured by Fedrigoni, Italy.

CONTENTS

- 7   Nina, who is still here
- 8   Ice
- 11   The Floods and the Frogs
- 12   In / Eleven Hours
- 13   Tulips
- 14   Morphine Driver
- 15   Still
- 16   My Parents' Accent
- 17   *Nonostante*
- 18   *Nevicata*
- 19   After she died
- 20   Folly
- 21   Dutch Elm
- 22   Lemon
- 23   Ajar
- 24   Hedgerow
- 25   Three ways to look at it
- 26   Varifocals
- 27   New Year's Day
- 28   Green
- 29   Collect
- 30   Backalong

- 32   ACKNOWLEDGEMENTS

for Nina

Nina, who is still here

> the green fields, neighbours to the churchyard,
> were as green as possible
>
> DOROTHY WORDSWORTH

She needs the greenth of it, green as the
grassy ease of it, the growth of trees; she's
greedy for these green leaves, these weeds,
she needs the fields, the beetle-breeze, to

see that she is real, that she is here

to see the gleam between the trees

she needs the grief of it, the green repeat of it,
to greet the leaves where she has been; she
needs the deep clean-green of it, the please –

the please, the grass, the ease of it.

Ice

I

                        so we
                  teach them
          there is more   much
          more below the surface
             and we hand them masks
though some are cracked and not everyone wants to look   the water is so cold
              down there   blind sharks two hundred
      years old move slow as thaw   the ice stroking
         fractured shadows over their scarred and ceaseless skin
           their spines   soft   still lengthening year on
              slow year   as   glaciers creak and calve
               searchlight slow   we keep one hand on the dark ice
     we descend unblinking   our pulses oil   water shifting in our ears
   there is more below the surface   the surface   gleams above us
     like a chandelier   like salt fire in the blue dark   look down
     we tell them   there is more
          there is more

   sleeper
     sharks

                                search

                                                search

light

               slow

II

you should have heard the noise   the stone made
chirruping   across   the ice   on the lake
like a message   through a wire clicking with starlings

so suddenly there and   lifted away
in the white air   fizzing like wings
I searched for more stones to hear it   again

and again   I can hear it like a voicemail
I'll play back sometimes   when   static   days
flicker   on hot stone   listening

for the dots and dashes   of swifts returning
I'll hear you   again   and your voices   and replay
your voices   flicking home   across   that   frozen   lake

III

Today I want to write about ice. How
things suspend in it. How light shines
through it into the eyes of my son
who has discovered he can capture this

with a camera. How yesterday I held
it up for him like a prism that burned
my hands. How it blazed in the flash.

But now the rain ticks on the window
and a friend is dying in hospital and
a sister slogs to the city for treatment
that may delay this for her a little longer

and in the place where he took the pictures
there is only a small skin of water
a dead leaf and a green one released from ice
and no sign warm fingers ever held a thing.

The Floods and the Frogs
SOMERSET SONNETS: 1

These fields were made for floods, the greener grass
an inch below the surface there. Each break
in winter cloud a flash of mirrored glass.
And backalong, frogs found that endless lake
and came, and came, and come again to spawn,
to claim the shallow greenlit world unseen.
But frogs and floods can't keep the grass for long.
The fields dry up. The tadpoles drown in weeds.
We dipped our hands and clutched at the soft slip,
the quickened light. We fumbled jars to heft
the dripping marbles to the stream. We tipped
them in and wished them well. And then we left.
Each year the frogs flood back and then they go.
They make the same mistakes. They never know.

In
Eleven Hours

this roof will tilt up out of a water
thick with silt and bitterness that glitters
just as pretty as it did this roof will shift under
the sun the magpie will come to sit as it did on the
tip and below the dripping eaves it will hear a slow hit
of dim water against this window and inside it will see these
books frilled floating falling open at pages no one has written and
when it lifts into a blue sky this roof will be a red island on a new map
lined with red islands and red islands and red islands and red islands and red

Tulips

There are tulips today
that she won't see, red
and yellow and blossom
on branches of apple.
The laburnum isn't
flowering yet. There are
daisies today. There are
small blue ones with
names I have forgotten
and tiny leaves. It is a blue
day that smells of earth.
I will plant geraniums
and busy lizzies that will
bloom until September,
and when that arrives
she will not be here.
I will plant them anyway,
for the pink and white
when I come home from
work, but she will still
be gone. I will plant them
anyway. She will still be
gone. I will fill the green
jug she gave me with
water and tulips. The sun
will move across the sky.

Morphine Driver

We could hear it was working from the soft shunt of fluid
through the tube and the reassuring whisper

she's fine, but we searched her face for the relief and found
cloud-clenched lids, thin-needled nothing and

today they are rehearsing for the airshow. The house is full
of the noise of nine planes, arrowheads and revolutions

though every time I look up there is an edge of a wing
or a tail of nothing or red smoke bleeding into a blue

that is full of just noise. A sky is a big place. Somewhere in here
there is a tiny panic at a window that might be closed or

a bee or not or a bluebottle trying to leave. A sky's a big place
and we will not believe in things we cannot see.

Still

So still the crickets come, brown bobbins,
pistoned, little cams on a grass-shaft.

So still they come
for shuttle, natter, laughter-rasp.

So still one answers my buzz
buzz for buzz from my shoe. Looks at me –

flicks kernel-quick into the yellow grass.
I am not what I said I was.

The geese disrupt uphill beautiful
the wind on the water on the ferns.

Kernels crack like skulls when the fire comes.
So still I hear the rasp and road behind me.

My Parents' Accent
SOMERSET SONNETS: 2

They sound like sun-warmed curves of hamstone now
to me. They sound like open fields and green
and blue. They whisper wisps of hay right down
the 303 behind an HGV.
They sound like shapes of hills, like bread, like sweet
inside a stalk, like rain on a brass band.
They sound like wooden spoons, like little leaps
in shiny shoes, like hands in pockets. And
with them, my voice sounds like that too. It rolls
in humming grass, unfurls and curls. It stays
a day or maybe two but it can't hold
and when they go, for good, that voice will fade
from me like green, like light, like cows that cried
in fields behind their house on August nights.

Nonostante

Again, I find myself saying this word. It stands
at the top of a garden with my grandfather
outlined against an Italian sky or an English one.
It speaks clearly into the yellow or white light,
the shaking heads of tall flowers. It starts
with the soft tenacity of *no*, of *no*, of two footsteps
on the doorstep, the echo there of *nostro, nonno,*
nevertheless. It is a step forward of a word,
a refusal to move, a promise to stay after all;
a withstanding, a standing, the clasp of
his steady brown hand underlined with soil.
He seeded these sounds in the garden, tying stalks
and cutting them, the star-shaped strawflowers
we called everlasting in dry bouquets in the shed,
the *nonno* we called Grandad who stood quietly
to enlist, to handle a gun he would never fire,
to surrender arms, to board the boat, to work,
to work, to say *I do* in English in a church
that wasn't his, to have his paper stamped,
to have his paper stamped, to have his paper
stamped. And despite it all, *tutti gli anni*, this word
that ends in tutting disapproval, it is a word
obstinate enough to take root, to lean into
the italics of the wind, to love regardless, to stand,
to grow paper-petalled stems the colours of the land.

Nevicata
SOMERSET SONNETS: 3

It snowed, one Somerset December, froze
the vines. He'd tried so hard to coax them up
the wall in English light. But he had stowed
his rhubarb wine, gold elderflower, sun-
bright sediment that warmed the cold back room
with glows and highs and pints of summers stashed
with elderberry, yellow plum. He scooped
a glass of snow, filled it with wine. It blushed
the crystal like a wedding, soaked into
the ice like love, old roses, pink as the
inside of bone. I ate it with a spoon,
not knowing all the words he'd handed me,
la neve fizzing on my tongue. *Nonno,
nevicare, nevicando,* snow, snow.

After she died

I started wearing gold hoops in my ears
like the women in my village did,
women with big arms and hard hands.

I found the small space above
people's faces and the quiet to the right
of the moon, and kept my eyes there.

I stacked books up to the surface,
hooked a highlighter between my fingers
the colour that coral used to be.

I bought a rug with an orange flower
and walked carefully around its soft edge
and curled my toes into its white centre.

I pressed my back into the old stones
of castles and the old stones of follies
that looked like castles, and stones.

I roasted chickens and ate the skin,
hot fat between my teeth, garlic
like a salve, like a spell.

I drive fast to folk songs, one hand
tight on the wheel, my left arm
outstretched like a huge single wing.

Folly

We talked about coming here together. We never did:
there's no picture of her in the window frame of the ruined
abbey, or on the bridge. She didn't pick up a pine cone.
I don't know if it would have been windy that day, cold, low
sun, if there would have been cygnets. There might have
been, and the wind might have raised rough lines of waves

that slipped towards us. This is a follied place. It built itself
on stories made from brick and plaster and didn't care if
they were true, air-shaped a temple and a tower because
it wanted them. Carve out the cave. Glitter it. Cast the statues.
Fix a tent in fibreglass. Flood the tileworks and call it a lake—
the fish won't know. They will be caught again, and put back.

I remember when we came here. There were twelve cygnets.
She stood in the window, and her hair flew around her face.

Dutch Elm
SOMERSET SONNETS: 4

My father used to talk about the elms
as if he walked among their standing ghosts.
As if he knew their green and lighted realm
was his, and let their wind-high voices float
to homelands he had never seen, in words
he didn't know. He mourned those trees for years.
He mourned them like the tongue he never heard
his father speak, the family that appeared
only in dreams. He knew the trees, at least.
He said that they were countless, then. He said
they stood like candle flames. But now new trees
stand in their place, and face the wind instead,
all voice and shade and green enough for us,
if we forget what we have lost or loved.

Lemon

For us
these are key, bright kindnesses
like teaspoons;
yellowmittens, a sharp morning
a warmer hand in the staffroom
or at the vets once, with an empty cage.
These squeezes, first-flutter easy, peasy as punch:

like the brief and everywhere drizzle
of lemon in that cake.

Ajar

Gone when I come home.
At first I don't notice, the sun
behind me flashed the same blood
orange, sparks of dust, no smithereen
sharp on the floor. They have swept it up. They
are sorry. It's only a thing. But when they are gone, where
do these solid things go? That spleen of bright ceramic that
was here? There are objects we inhabit, that do not leave. That
heavy ring, three garnets, tiny diamonds I could pull out of the
air. That fibre-optic lamp, its stroke of stars; that velvet-green
jacket. That marbled mermaid book. This ginger jar. And so
there is a space that holds its shape, its curve, the light still
bends around it, the loose lid rattles like a gift. There is a
sort of shine there still, a freckle of air that feels like
shine, where gold paint circled curls of flowers,
and still a fleeting wink of marigold, tiger,
every time I come home, between the
sparks, in the space I occupy now,
the space where you stand in
the light from the open door.

Hedgerow
SOMERSET SONNETS: 5

Two ways to do it: lopping, or laying.
The blade is quick as miles but leaves behind
a scream of bone-white splinters, ratchetings
of birds into a cold and lidless sky.
But laying brings a knife to nick the boughs,
the time to ease them down, plant woven stakes,
work twenty metres in a day to grout
the slow tilework of fields. A hedge will wait.
And braided life remains in layers then,
like ours. The birds can pick their way inside
a smaller hazel world that grows and smells
the same, where eggs are screened in dim green light,
in soft strata of leaves. And soon the frost
will retreat, and time and nothing is lost.

Three ways to look at it

1

The end. No one speaks
of her and there are party
games and ten! nine! eight!
to a new year that does not
have her in it.

2

Never the bloody end.
She's missing from
all our party games,
all our new years shouting
seven! six! five! four!

3

Two! one! Never the end.
We think of her. One day,
it will be all of us.
There will be new years.
There will be party games.

Varifocals

And it all appears, the long and short of it,
as if there is no footnote so small

that a movement of my eyes can't
sharpen it, no cloudscape so distant

and formless I can't bring it into clean
relief with a turn of my head. And I can see

now that my watch has a tiny window
to hold the date, and that it's wrong.

I can see the precision of a cirrus sky
and the peeling blue of the front door,

pick eggshell specks out of the cake mix.
I can read closer than arm's length, now.

I can see the old cat's clouded yellow eyes,
the eye of the needle first time, neat stitches,

the running fox and the kite and the kite.
Hallmarks, and pockmarks. Washing labels;

window dust. I walk in the wind and my eyes
move in my face, my head swivels like a lamp –

sparrow, cloud, pylon, puddle, shoe, distant
figure. I tilt my chin to look at you.

New Year's Day

It feels late to begin. The sun is high.
The children are still in gangly sleep.

Debussy said the important notes
are the ones you let fall under the table.

Under this table, crumbs, a pencil,
a discarded ten of hearts. I find

Debussy never said that. Who did?
I don't listen to Debussy these days.
It's late and I want all the notes.

Green
SOMERSET SONNETS: 6

We needed spotted dock leaves for our stings;
pulled fists of cobnuts, ropes of sticky weed
and buttercups to shove under our chins
in conkered fields. We needed weeping trees
for seeking, dandelions for the time;
we nicked and chained the days with brambled thumbs,
wove clover crowns. We found the grass that whined,
the grass to suck, the grass that would draw blood.
We knew never to touch the yew or dead
man's fingers; foxgloves, rhubarb, mistletoe;
steered clear of honeysuckle, cuckoo spit.
We knew to leave the unripe things alone.
The rest was cow parsley and weeds and stuff:
green things we didn't need. We knew enough.

Collect

When they arrived it was like orcas had arrived
in the room, or sea lions, or emperor penguins,
perhaps, because it's not like penguins are
threatening but those things are bigger

than you think, and if they walked quietly
into your house and stood there it would be weird,
especially if three or four of them rocked up,
implausibly large in their smart black suits, taking up

the space that was left in the spring quiet
of a Sunday morning in the living room with the
dog and the cartoons and the children in pyjamas
and the daffodils and the hospital bed, and they

took her, and they said that they were sorry.
After they left, the house rolled over like a wave.

She gave me beautiful cards of collective nouns once.
There was a pod, a herd, a huddle, a wake, a raft.

Backalong
SOMERSET SONNETS: 7

We never need to know how long ago
it was. It happened backalong. It was,
then. It has been. There's comfort in the close
and far of those soft vaguenesses, the years
or hours ago, the Spring, the war, the Spring,
those Christmases, or when he said he'd stay
or when they built the Tor, or crowned a king,
or made the songs, the laws, the motorway.
And backalong keeps all these things behind
a gently locked glass door. Their shapes are blurred
inside. It doesn't matter when. She died
backalong. See? Backalong, ice covered
the Earth. Backalong, one hot afternoon,
she walked fast through the grass to feel it move.

ACKNOWLEDGEMENTS

Warm thanks to the editors of the publications in which some of these poems first appeared: *Bad Lilies, The Friday Poem, The Interpreter's House, Poetry News, Red Ogre Review* and the *Winchester Poetry Prize anthology 2022*. 'Varifocals' was selected as the winner of the Hamish Canham Prize for 2023/2024. 'Nina, who is still here' was Highly Commended in the Winchester Poetry Prize 2022 and 'After she died' was longlisted in the *Mslexia* Poetry Competition.

Sincere appreciation to the tutors who were so instrumental in challenging and supporting me during my MA with Lancaster University: Conor O'Callaghan, Sarah Corbett, Paul Farley and Eoghan Walls. Love and gratitude to all the cheerleader poets I've met along the way, who have given me advice and encouragement for no reason at all other than their loveliness: Ellora Sutton, Harriet Truscott, Jacob Ramirez, Kathryn Bevis, Christina Lloyd, Attie Lime, David Day (not the Canadian one!), Holly Corfield Carr, Alexandra Corrin-Tachibana, Matthew M.C. Smith and the fantastic #TopTweetTuesday poets. Thanks also to Kim Moore and Clare Shaw for their January Writing Hours in which several of these poems were conceived, and Liz Berry whose workshop 'Treasuring your Word Hoard' for the Winchester Poetry Festival kickstarted the poem 'Backalong' and found me my title. Thank goodness for Jo Bell, who is exactly the fizzing and forthright mentor I need.

I am indebted to Arts Council England for DYCP funding that enables me to pursue these opportunities, and to Painshill Park in Cobham for a year-long residency that inspired several of these poems and is an absolute joy.

A huge thank you to Imtiaz Dharker, the *Mslexia* team, Bloodaxe Books and Neil Astley for making this happen.

Thank you to the marvellous Hannah Bavin, the other head of our English Department Hydra, who took on far more than 50% of the job while I was writing this, and to Poetry Club who inspire me every Friday without fail and eat all my sweets. I am beyond grateful to Mary Grist, Sara Sheldrake, Becky Spillett and Holly Sykes: beautiful writers, eagle-eyed readers, relentless supporters, wonderful friends.

To Drew, thank you.

And to Pop, without whom the MA and all of this would never have happened, to my family, who were proud even backalong, to Annie, Elliot and Steve, who are everything: love you, thank you.